About the author

JAMES P. CANNON, who died at age eighty-four in August of 1974, devoted his entire adult life to the labor and socialist movements. He was an organizer and agitator for the Industrial Workers of the World, a member of the left wing of the Socialist Party before World War I, and a founder of the American Communist Party. Expelled from the CP in 1928 for his opposition to Stalinism, he went on to collaborate with Leon Trotsky in the founding of the Fourth International in 1938. At the time of his death he was the national chairman emeritus of the Socialist Workers Party.

A selected reading list of James P. Cannon's most important published works on party building can be found on page 19.

The revolutionary party
Its role in the struggle for socialism

The greatest contribution to the arsenal of Marxism since the death of Engels in 1895 was Lenin's conception of the vanguard party as the organizer and director of the proletarian revolution. That celebrated theory of organization was not, as some contend, simply a product of the special Russian conditions of his time and restricted to them. It is deep-rooted in two of the weightiest realities of the twentieth century: the *actuality* of the workers' struggle for the conquest of power, and the *necessity* of creating a leadership capable of carrying it through to the end.

Recognizing that our epoch was characterized by imperialist wars, proletarian revolutions, and colonial uprisings, Lenin deliberately set out at the beginning of this century to form a party able to turn such cataclysmic events to the advantage of socialism. The triumph of the Bolsheviks in the upheavals of 1917, and the durability of the Soviet Union they established, attested to Lenin's foresight and the merits of his methods of organization. His party stands out as the unsurpassed prototype of what a democratic and centralized leadership of the workers, true to

Marxist principles and applying them with courage and skill, can be and do.

Limited as it was to a single country, the epoch-making achievement of the Bolsheviks did not conclusively dispose of further dispute over the nature of the revolutionary leadership. That controversy has continued ever since. Fifty years afterwards there is no lack of skeptics inside the socialist ranks who doubt or deny that a party of the Leninist type is either necessary or desirable. And even where Lenin's theory is clearly understood and convincing, the problem of the vanguard party remains as urgent as ever, since it has yet to be solved in the everyday struggle against the old order.

A correct appreciation of the vanguard party and its indispensable role depends upon understanding the crucial importance of the subjective factors in the proletarian revolution. On a broad historical scale, and in the final accounting, economic conditions are decisive in shaping the development of society. This truth of historical materialism does not negate the fact that the political and psychological processes unfolding within the working masses more directly and immediately affect the course, the pace, and the outcome of the national and world revolution. Once the objective material preconditions for revolutionary activity by the workers have reached a certain point of maturity, their will and consciousness, expressed through the intervention of the organized vanguard, can become the key component in determining the outcome of the class struggle.

The Leninist theory of the vanguard party is based on two factors: the heterogeneity of the working class and the exceptionally conscious character of the movement for socialism. The revolutionizing of the proletariat and oppressed people in general is a complex, prolonged, and contradictory affair. Under class society and capitalism, the toilers are stratified and divided in many ways; they live under very dissimilar conditions and are at disparate stages of economic and political development. Their culture is inadequate and their outlook narrow.

Consequently they do not and cannot all at once, en masse and to the same degree, arrive at a clear and comprehensive understanding of their real position in society or the political course they must follow to end the evils they suffer from and make their way to a better system. Still less can they learn quickly and easily how to act most effectively to protect and promote their class interests.

This irregular self-determination of the class as a whole is the primary cause for a vanguard party. It has to be constituted by those elements of the class and their spokesmen who grasp the requirements for revolutionary action and proceed to their implementation sooner than the bulk of the proletariat on both a national and international scale. Here also is the basic reason that the vanguard always begins as a minority of its class, a "splinter group." The earliest formations of advanced workers committed to socialism, and their intellectual associates propagating its views, must first organize themselves around a definite body of scientific doctrine, class tradition, and experience, and work out a correct political program in order then to organize and lead the big battalions of revolutionary forces.

The vanguard party should aim at all times to reach, move, and win the broadest masses. Yet, beginning with Lenin's Bolsheviks, no such party has ever started out with the backing of the majority of the class and as its recognized head. It originates, as a rule, as a group of propagandists concerned with the elaboration and dissemination of ideas. It trains, teaches, and tempers cadres around that program and outlook which they take to the masses for consideration, adoption, action, and verification.

The size and influence of their organization is never a matter of indifference to serious revolutionists. Nonetheless, *quantitative* indices alone cannot be taken as the decisive determinants for judging the real nature of a revolutionary grouping. More fundamental are such qualitative features as the program and relationship with the class whose interests it formulates, represents, and fights for.

"The interests of the class cannot be formulated otherwise than in the shape of a program; the program cannot be defended otherwise than by creating the party," wrote Trotsky in *What Next?* "The class, taken by itself, is only raw material for exploitation. The proletariat acquires an independent role only at that moment when, from a social class *in itself,* it becomes a political class *for itself.* This cannot take place otherwise than through the medium of a party. The party is that historical organ by means of which the class becomes class conscious."

Marxism teaches that the revolution against capitalism and the socialist reconstruction of the old world can be accomplished only through conscious, collective action by the workers themselves. The vanguard party is the highest expression and irreplaceable instrument of that class consciousness at all stages of the world revolutionary process. In the prerevolutionary period the vanguard assembles and welds together the cadres who march ahead of the main army but seek at all points to maintain correct relations with it. The vanguard grows in numbers and influence and comes to the fore in the course of the mass struggle for supremacy which it aspires to bring to a successful conclusion. After the overthrow of the old ruling powers, the vanguard leads the people in the tasks of defending and constructing the new society.

A political organization capable of handling such colossal tasks cannot arise spontaneously or haphazardly; *it has to be continuously, consistently, and consciously built.* It is not only foolish but fatal to take a lackadaisical attitude toward party-building or its problems. The bitter experiences of so many revolutionary opportunities aborted, mismanaged, and ruined over the past half century by inadequate or treacherous leaderships has incontestably demonstrated that nonchalance in this vital area is a sure formula for disorientation and defeat.

Lenin's superb capacities as a revolutionary leader were best shown in his insistence upon the utmost consciousness in all aspects of party-building, from capital issues of theory and policy to the meticulous attention given to small details of daily work. Other parties and kinds of parties are content to amble and stumble along, dealing empirically and in a makeshift manner with problems as they arise. Lenin introduced system and planning into the construction and activity of the revolutionary party on the road to power, not only into the economy such a party was later called upon to direct. He left as little as possible to chance and improvisation. Proceeding from a formulated appraisal of the given stage of the struggle, he singled out the main tasks at hand and sought to discover and devise the best ways and means of solving them in accord with the long-range goals of world socialism.

The vanguard party, guided by the methods of scientific socialism and totally dedicated to the welfare of the toiling masses and all victims of oppression, must always be in principled opposition to the guardians and institutions of class society. These traits can immunize it against the infections, and armor it against the pressures, of alien class influences. But the Leninist party must be, above all, a *combat* party intent on organizing the masses for effective action leading to the taking of power.

That overriding aim determines the character of the party and priority of its tasks. It cannot be a talking shop for aimless and endless debate. The purpose of its deliberations, discussions, and internal disputes is to arrive at decisions for action and systematic work. Neither can it be an infirmary for the care and cure of sick souls, nor itself a model of the future socialist society. It is a band of revolutionary fighters, ready, willing, and able to meet and defeat all enemies of the people and assist the masses in clearing the way to the new world.

Much of the New Left, imbued with an anarchistic or existentialist spirit, denigrate or dismiss professional leadership in a revolutionary movement. So do some disillusioned workers and ex-radicals, who have come to equate conscientious dedication to full-time leadership with bureaucratic domination and privilege. They fail to understand the interrelations between the masses, the revolutionary class, the party, and its leadership. Just as the revolutionary class leads the nation forward, so the vanguard party leads the class. However, the role of leadership does not stop there. The party itself needs leadership. It is impossible for a revolutionary party to provide correct leadership without the right sort of leaders. This leadership performs the same functions within the vanguard party as that party does for the working class.

Its cadres remain the backbone of the party, in periods of contraction as well as expansion. The vitality of such a party is certified by the capacity to extend and replenish its cadres and reproduce qualified leaders from one generation to another.

The vanguard party cannot be proclaimed by sectarian fiat or be created overnight. Its leadership and membership are selected and sifted out by tests and trials in the mass movement, and in the internal controversies and sharp conflicts over the critical policy questions raised at every turn in the class struggle. It is not possible to step over, and even less possible to leap over, the preliminary stage in which the basic cadres of the party organize and reorganize themselves in preparation for, and in connection with, the larger job of organizing and winning over broad sections of the masses.

The decisive role that kind of party can play in the making of history was dramatically exemplified by the Bolshevik cadres in the first world war and the first proletarian revolution. These cadres degenerated or were destroyed and replaced after Lenin's death by the totalitarian apparatus of the Soviet bureaucracy fashioned under Stalin. The importance of such cadres was negatively confirmed by the terrible defeats of the socialist forces in other countries, extending from the Germany of 1918 to the Spain of 1936–1939, because of the opportunism, defects, or defaults of the labor leaderships.

Contrary to the opinions of some other students of his remarkable career, I believe that Trotsky's most valuable contribution to the world revolutionary movement in the struggle against Stalinism and centrism was his defense and enrichment of the Leninist principles of the party, culminating in the decision to create new parties of the Fourth International along these lines. Trotsky was from 1903 to 1917 opposed in theory and practice to Lenin's methods of building a revolutionary party. It is a tribute to his exemplary objectivity and capacity for growth that he wholeheartedly came over to Lenin's conceptions in 1917, when he saw them verified by the developments of the revolution at home and abroad.

From that point to his last day Trotsky never for a moment wavered in his adherence to these methods of party-building. After correcting his mistake in that department, he became, after Lenin's death in 1924, the foremost exponent and developer of the Bolshevik traditions of the vanguard party in national and international politics.

Most people think that Trotsky's genius was best displayed in his work as theorist of the permanent revolution, as the head of the October uprising, or as creator and commander of the Red Army. I believe that he exercised his powers of revolutionary Marxist leadership most eminently not during the rise but during the recession of the Russian and world revolutions, when, as leader of the Left Opposition, he undertook to save the program and perspectives of the Bolshevik Party against the Stalinist reaction, and then founded the Fourth International once the Comintern had decisively disclosed its bankruptcy in 1933. The purpose of the new International was to create and coordinate new revolutionary mass parties of the world working class.

Trotsky summarized his views on the momentous importance of the vanguard party in the transitional program he drafted for its founding congress in 1938. He asserted that "the historical crisis of mankind is reduced to the crisis of the revolutionary leadership." The principal strategic task for our whole epoch is "overcoming the contradiction between the maturity of objective revolutionary conditions and the immaturity of the proletariat and its vanguard (the confusion and disappointment of the older generation, the inexperience of the younger generation).”

He pointed out that the vanguard party was the sole agency by which this burning political problem of the imperialist phase of world capitalism could be solved. More specifically, he stated categorically: “. . . the crisis of the proletarian leadership, having become the crisis in mankind’s culture, can be resolved only by the Fourth International,” the World Party of the Socialist Revolution.

Have the major experiences in the struggle for socialism, since this was written, spoken for or against Trotsky’s pregnant political generalizations? Has the crisis of mankind, or the crisis of the proletarian leadership, been overcome?

The fact is it has grown ever deeper and more acute with the advent of nuclear weapons and the failures of the established parties to overthrow capitalist imperialism and promote the progress of socialism.

In the revolutionary resurgence in Western Europe opened by Mussolini’s deposition in July 1943, which signalized the eclipse of fascism, to the ousting of the Communists from the coalition cabinets in France and Italy in 1947, the Stalinist and Social Democratic parties repeated their previous treachery and impotence by refusing to pursue a revolutionary policy directed toward the conquest of power in a highly revolutionary situation. These defaults and defeats permitted capitalism to be restabilized in the second most important sector of that system.

In the colonial countries from 1945 on, Communist leaderships, handcuffed or misled by Kremlin diplomacy, have been responsible for many setbacks and disasters. These have stretched from the compromise of the Indochinese Communists with the French imperialists in 1945 to political subservience to such representatives of the “progressive” bourgeoisie as Nehru in India, Kassim in Iraq, Goulart in Brazil, and Sukarno in Indonesia. The terrible reverses of the colonial freedom struggle, culminating in the Indonesian butchery of 1965, owing to such false leadership, provide powerful evidence that the need for new and better leadership is as urgent in the "Third World" as elsewhere.

The conquest of power by the Communist parties of Yugoslavia, China, North Korea, and North Vietnam has induced not a few radicals and ex-Trotskyists to assume or assert that Lenin's teachings on the party, and Trotsky's reaffirmation of them, are out of date. These developments prove, they argue, that it is a waste of time, a useless undertaking, to try to build independent revolutionary parties of the Leninist type as Trotsky advised, since the exploiters can be overthrown with other kinds of parties, especially if these are supported by a powerful workers' state like the Soviet Union or China.

What substance do these arguments have? It should first be observed that Trotsky himself foresaw and allowed for such a possibility. In the "Transitional Program" he wrote: ". . . one cannot categorically deny in advance the theoretical possibility that, under the influence of completely exceptional circumstances (war, defeat, financial crash, mass revolutionary pressure, etc.), the petty-bourgeois parties including the Stalinists may go further than they themselves wish along the road to a break with the bourgeoisie."

In the postwar years these exceptional conditions in the more backward countries have been the prostration and collapse of the most corrupt colonial bourgeoisies, the weaknesses of the old imperialist powers in Europe and of Japan, and the mighty upsurge of the indigenous peasant and proletarian masses. Certain Communist leaderships were confronted with the alternatives of being crushed by reaction, outflanked by the revolutionary forces, or taking command of the national liberation and anticapitalist struggles. After some hesitation and vacillation, and against the Kremlin's advice, the Communist leaders in Yugoslavia, China, and Vietnam took the latter course and led the proletariat and peasantry to power.

In its resolution on "The Dynamics of World Revolution Today," adopted at the 1963 Reunification Congress, the Fourth

International has taken into account this variant of political development as follows: "The weakness of the enemy in the backward countries has opened the possibility of coming to power with a blunted instrument."

However, this factual observation does not dispose of the entire question, or even touch its most important aspects. The deformations of the regimes emanating from the revolutionary movements headed by the Stalinized parties, and the opportunism and sectarianism exhibited by their leaderships since assuming power, notably in Eastern Europe, Yugoslavia, and China, demonstrate that the need for organizing genuine Marxist parties is not ended with the overthrow of capitalist domination. The building of such political formations can become equally urgent as the result of the bureaucratic degeneration and deformation of postcapitalist states in an environment where imperialism remains predominant and backwardness prevails.

This was first recognized in the case of the Soviet Union by Trotsky in 1933. That political conclusion retains full validity for all those workers' states governed by parties that fail to uphold or foster a democratic internal regime or pursue an international revolutionary line. The experience of the Polish and Hungarian uprisings of 1956, and restriction of the de-Stalinization processes in the Soviet Union, alike demonstrate the need for an independent Marxist-Leninist party to lead the antibureaucratic revolution to the end.

The keynote of the reunification document is that "the building of new mass revolutionary parties remains the central strategic task" in all three sectors of the international struggle for socialism: the workers' states, the colonial regions, and above all in the advanced capitalisms.

If Yugoslavia and China are cited to show that any party will do in a pinch, the example of Cuba is often brought forward as proof that no party at all is required in the struggle for power, or that any kind of improvised political outfit will do the job. First of all, this involves a misconstruction of the political history of the Cuban Revolution. The July 26 Movement had a small, close-knit nucleus of leaders, subjected to military discipline by the imperatives of armed combat. They had to construct a broader leadership in the heat of civil war against Batista. Once the Cuban freedom fighters had become sovereign in the country, they found not only that they could not dispense with a vanguard party, but that they desperately needed one. They have therefore proceeded to construct one along Marxist lines and are still engaged in that task nine years after their victory.

Wouldn't their difficulties have been lessened before and after the taking of power if they had been able to enter the revolution with a more powerful cadre and party? But the default of the Cuban Stalinists foreclosed that more favorable possibility. Moreover, it should be recognized that, since the Cuban experience, both the imperialists and their native satellites under Washington's direction are much more alerted and prompt to take repressive measures to nip rebellion in the bud.

The circumstances of the struggle for power in the highly industrialized countries are vastly different from those in colonial lands, where the native upper classes are feeble, isolated, and discredited, and where the impetus of the unsolved tasks of the democratic revolution reinforces the claims of the wage workers. It would be foolish and fatal to hold that the workers in the imperialist strongholds will be able to get rid of capitalism under the direction of the bureaucratized, corrupt, and ossified Social Democratic or Communist parties, or any centrist shadow of them. Here the injunction to build revolutionary Marxist parties is absolutely unconditional.

The difficulties encountered by the Trotskyist vanguard over the past three decades show that there are no easy or simple recipes for solving the multiple problems posed by this necessity. The major obstacle to building alternative leaderships in most of these countries is the presence of powerful and wealthy Labor, Social Democratic, or Communist organizations which exercise bureaucratic control over the labor movement, but for traditional reasons continue to exact a certain loyalty from the workers. Under such conditions it is often advisable for the original corps of revolutionary Marxists to enter and work for extended periods within such mass parties.

It should never for a moment be forgotten that the prime objective of such a tactical entry is the creation, consolidation, and expansion of the initial cadres and the growth of ties with the most advanced elements. It is not an end in itself. The immediate aim is to transform a propaganda group into a force capable of influencing, organizing, and directing broad masses in action. The ultimate goal is to create a new mass party of the working class along this road.

Experience has shown that there are many pitfalls in implementing an entrist tactic. As a result of prolonged immersion in reformist work and overadaptation to a centrist environment, the fiber of the revolutionary cadre may become corroded and its perspectives dimmed and even lost. Total immersion in such a milieu has many liabilities and dangers. It is therefore essential that entrist work be complemented by a sector of open public work through which the full program and policies of the Fourth International can at all times be made accessible to the advanced workers.

It is also possible (We have seen such cases!) for entrism to be conducted in an impatient and inflexible way. Then, when adequate results are not quickly forthcoming, the group can prematurely revert to an independent organizational status. If persisted in, such a sectarian course can, under cover of a falsetto ultraleft rhetoric, lead to self-isolation and impotence. It can help the reformist and Communist bureaucrats by leaving them in uncontested command of the situation and narrowing the channels of contact and communication between the revolutionary Marxists and the best militants in the traditional parties.

Both through independent or entrist activities, as the given situation warranted, the American Trotskyists have been busy building a revolutionary Marxist party in the United States ever since they discarded the prospect of reforming the Communist Party in 1933. The Socialist Workers Party regards itself as the legitimate inheritor of the finest traditions of the Socialist movement of Debs, the Socialist Labor Party of De Leon, the IWW of St. John and Haywood, and the early Communist Party. It has drawn upon and benefited from the good and bad experiences of these pioneer attempts to create the party needed by the American workers to lead their revolution.

The history of American communism since its inception in 1919 has been a record of struggle for the right kind of party. All the other problems have been related to this central issue.

Everything that has been done since October 1917 for the advancement of socialism in this citadel of world capitalism and counterrevolution has been governed by this necessity of building the vanguard party, and whatever will be accomplished in the future will, in my opinion, revolve around it. The key to the victory of socialism in the United States will be the fusion of American power, above all the potential power of its working class, with Russian ideas, first and foremost the organizational principles of Lenin's Bolshevism.

The Leninist party proved indispensable in Russia, where the belated bourgeoisie was a feeble social and political force. It will be a million times more necessary in America, the home of the strongest, richest, and most ruthless exploiting class. The Bolshevik conception of the party and its leadership originated and was first put to the test in the weakest and most backward of capitalist countries. I venture to predict that it will become naturalized and find its fullest application in the struggle for socialism in the most developed country of capitalism.

The revolutionists here confront the most highly organized concentration of economic, political, military, and cultural power in history. These mighty forces of reaction cannot and will not be overthrown without a movement of the popular masses, black and white, which has a centralized, disciplined, principled, experienced Marxist leadership at its head.

It is impossible to stumble into a successful revolution in the United States. It will have to be organized and directed by people and a party that have at their command all the theory, knowledge, resources, and lessons accumulated by the world working class. Its know-how and organization in politics and action must match and surpass that of its enemies.

Those who claim that a Leninist party is irrelevant or unneeded in the advanced capitalisms are 100 per cent wrong. On the contrary, such a party is an absolutely essential condition and instrument for the promotion and triumph of the socialist revolution in the United States, the paragon of world capitalism. Just as the overturn inaugurated by the Bolsheviks under Lenin and Trotsky in 1917 was the first giant step in the world socialist revolution and renovation, so the Leninist theory of the party, first vindicated by that event, will find its ultimate verification in the overthrow of imperialism in its central fortress and the establishment of a socialist regime with full democracy on American soil.

Nothing less than the fate of humanity hinges upon the speediest solution of the drawn-out crisis of proletarian leadership. This will have to be done under the banner and through the program of the parties of the Fourth International. The very physical existence of our species depends upon the prompt fulfillment of this supreme obligation. No greater task was ever shouldered by revolutionists of the Marxist school—and not too much time will be given by the monopolists and militarists at bay to carry it through.

On this fiftieth anniversary of the imperishable October Revolution, which has shaped and changed all our lives, our motto is: "To work with more energy toward that goal and win it for the good of mankind."

James P. Cannon on party building

The main written legacy left by James P. Cannon to the revolutionary movement is on party building. The following selection includes his most important published contributions on this subject.

1. Introduction
"Tribute to James P. Cannon"
   Speech by Joseph Hansen in Oberlin, Ohio.
   Printed in the *Militant,* Sept. 6, 1974

2. The origins of American Trotskyism
"The Beginning of the Left Opposition"
   Chapter III of *History of American Trotskyism.*
"The First Ten Years in Perspective"
   Introduction of *The First Ten Years of American Communism.*

3. Mass work/fusion with another party
"The Turn to Mass Work"
   Chapter VII of *History of American Trotskyism.*
"The Great Minneapolis Strikes"
   Chapter VIII of *History of American Trotskyism.*
"The Fusion with the Musteites"
   Chapter IX of *History of American Trotskyism.*

4. Defense policy
"Political Principles and Propaganda Methods
   Cannon's reply to Grandizo Munis's criticism of SWP
   defense policy in the Minneapolis trial. Printed in *Socialism on Trial,* 1973 edition.

5. Election policy
"Election Policy in 1948"
> Cannon's report to the February 1948 plenum of the
> National Committee of the SWP. Printed in *Aspects of
> Socialist Election Policy*, an Education for Socialists Bulletin
> published by the Education Dept. of the SWP.

6. Party building in a period of expansion
Excerpts from *Letters from Prison* on:
Education of cadres—pp 65–77, 285–287, 295–296
Finances—pp 132–133
Leadership—pp 17, 201–205, 209–236, 288–289, 301
Party expansion—pp 109–110, 112–113, 243–246, 253–255
Party press—pp 29, 34, 63–64, 113–114, 114, 122–123, 134–
> 135, 154, 172–173, 234, 261–262, 264–266, 266–269,
> 270–274, 301, 303–305
Youth—p. 298

7. Internationalism
"The End of the Comintern and the Prospects of Labor Interna-
> tionalism"—Speech by Cannon in New York City, May 30,
> 1943. Printed in *Speeches for Socialism.*
"Internationalism and the SWP"
> Speech to meeting of majority caucus in New York Local of
> SWP during Cochran fight, May 18, 1953. Printed in
> *Speeches to the Party.*

8. Struggles against revisionism
"Struggle for a Proletarian Party"
> Essay by Cannon on organizational lessons to be drawn
> from fight with the Shachtmanites in 1939–40. Printed in
> *Struggle for a Proletarian Party.*
"Trade Unionists and Revolutionists"
> Speech by Cannon during Cochran fight in SWP. Delivered
> at meeting of the majority caucus of New York Local, May

11, 1953. Printed in *Speeches to the Party*.
"Factional Struggle and Party Leadership"
  Speech by Cannon to SWP National Committee, Nov. 3,
  1953. Printed in *Speeches to the Party*.

9. Visions of the socialist future
"What Socialist America Will Look Like"
  Printed in *America's Road to Socialism*.

History of American Trotskyism 1928–38
Report of a Participant
JAMES P. CANNON

In twelve talks given in 1944 Cannon recounts the early efforts by communists in the U.S. to build a new kind of proletarian party. It carries the story from the first steps forward by vanguard workers politically responding to the victory of the October 1917 Russian Revolution up to the eve of World War II when the communist organization in the U.S. takes the name Socialist Workers Party. With a new preface by Jack Barnes. Also in French and Spanish. $22

The Changing Face of U.S. Politics
Working-Class Politics and the Unions
JACK BARNES

Building the kind of party the working class needs to prepare for coming class battles—battles through which they will revolutionize themselves, their unions, and all of society. It is a handbook for workers, farmers, and youth repelled by the social inequalities, economic instability, racism, women's oppression, cop violence, and wars endemic to capitalism . . . and who are determined to overturn that exploitative system. $23.00

JACK BARNES
THE CHANGING FACE OF U.S. POLITICS
Working-class politics and the unions

Lenin's Final Fight
Speeches and Writings, 1922–23
V.I. LENIN

In the early 1920s Lenin waged a political battle in the Communist Party leadership in the USSR to maintain the course that had enabled workers and peasants to overthrow the tsarist empire, carry out the first socialist revolution, and begin building a world communist movement. The issues posed in this fight—from the leadership's class composition, to the worker-peasant alliance and battle against national oppression—remain central to world politics today. $19.95 Also in Spanish.

The First Ten Years of American Communism
A Participant's Account
JAMES P. CANNON

"Stalinism has worked mightily to obliterate the honorable record of American communism in its pioneer days. Yet the Communist Party wrote such a chapter too, and the young militants of the new generation ought to know about it and claim it for their own. It belongs to them." — James P. Cannon, 1962. $19.95

New International

A MAGAZINE OF MARXIST POLITICS AND THEORY

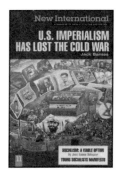

New International no. 11

U.S. Imperialism Has Lost the Cold War *by Jack Barnes* • Socialism: A Viable Option *by José Ramón Balaguer* • Young Socialists Manifesto • The Communist Strategy of Party Building Today *by Mary-Alice Waters* • Ours Is the Epoch of World Revolution *by Jack Barnes and Mary-Alice Waters* $14.00

New International no. 10

Imperialism's March toward Fascism and War *by Jack Barnes* • What the 1987 Stock Market Crash Foretold • Defending Cuba, Defending Cuba's Socialist Revolution *by Mary-Alice Waters* $14.00

New International no. 8

The Politics of Economics: Che Guevara and Marxist Continuity *by Steve Clark and Jack Barnes* • Che's Contribution to the Cuban Economy *by Carlos Rafael Rodríguez* • On the Concept of Value *and* The Meaning of Socialist Planning, two articles *by Ernesto Che Guevara* $10.00

New International no. 7

Opening Guns of World War III: Washington's Assault on Iraq *by Jack Barnes* • 1945: When U.S. Troops Said "No!" *by Mary-Alice Waters* • Lessons from the Iran-Iraq War *by Samad Sharif* $12.00

Distributed by Pathfinder

Most of these articles are also available in Spanish in *Nueva Internacional*, and in French in *Nouvelle Internationale*. Some are also available in Swedish in *Ny International*.

from Pathfinder

Capitalism's World Disorder
Working-Class Politics at the Millennium
JACK BARNES

The social devastation and financial panic,
the coarsening of politics and politics of resentment, the
cop brutality and acts of imperialist aggression
accelerating around us—all are the product of lawful
forces unleashed by capitalism. But the future the
propertied classes have in store for us can be changed by
the united struggle and selfless action
of workers and farmers conscious of their power
to transform the world. $23.95. Also available in Spanish
and French.

Their Trotsky and Ours
JACK BARNES

History shows that small revolutionary organizations will
face not only the test of wars and repression, but also
potentially shattering opportunities that emerge
unexpectedly when strikes and social struggles explode. As
that happens, communist parties recruit, fuse with other
workers organizations and grow into mass proletarian
parties contesting to lead workers and farmers to power.
This assumes that their cadres have absorbed a world
communist program, are proletarian in life and work,
and have forged a leadership with an acute sense of what
to do next. *Their Trotsky and Ours* is about building such
parties. Also in French and Spanish. $15

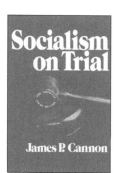

Socialism on Trial
JAMES P. CANNON

The basic ideas of socialism, explained in testimony during the
trial of 18 leaders of the Minneapolis Teamsters union and the
Socialist Workers Party framed up and imprisoned under the
notorious Smith "Gag" Act during World War II. $15.95

The Communist Manifesto

KARL MARX AND FREDERICK ENGELS
Founding document of the modern working-class movement,
published in 1848. Explains why communism is derived not from
preconceived principles but from facts, from proletarian
movements springing from the actual class struggle. $3.95.
Also available in Spanish.

Pathfinder Was Born
with the October Revolution

MARY-ALICE WATERS
Pathfinder Press traces an unbroken continuity to the pioneering
forces who launched the world effort to defend and emulate the
first socialist revolution—the October 1917 revolution in
Russia. From the writings of Marx, Engels, Lenin, and Trotsky, to
the words of Malcolm X, Fidel Castro, and Che Guevara, to those
of James P. Cannon, Farrell Dobbs, and leaders of the
communist movement in the U.S. today, Pathfinder books aim to
"advance the understanding, confidence, and combativity of
working people." $3.00. Also available in Spanish and French.

Che Guevara Talks to Young People

The legendary Argentine-born revolutionary challenges youth of
Cuba and the world to work and become disciplined. To
fearlessly join the front lines of struggles, small and large.
To read and to study. To aspire to be revolutionary combatants.
To politicize the organizations they are part of and in the
process politicize themselves. To become a different kind of
human being as they strive together with working people of all
lands to transform the world. And, along this line of march,
to renew and revel in the spontaneity and joy of being young.
$14.95. Also available in Spanish.

To Speak the Truth

Why Washington's 'Cold War'
against Cuba Doesn't End

FIDEL CASTRO AND CHE GUEVARA
In historic speeches before the United Nations and UN bodies,
Guevara and Castro address the workers of the world,
explaining why the U.S. government so hates the example set by
the socialist revolution in Cuba and why Washington's effort to
destroy it will fail. $16.95

Malcolm X Speaks

Speeches from the last year of Malcolm X's life tracing the evolution of his views on racism, capitalism, socialism, political action, and more. $17.95. Also available in Spanish.

U.S. Hands off the Mideast!

Cuba Speaks out at the United Nations

FIDEL CASTRO, RICARDO ALARCON

The case against Washington's 1990–91 embargo and war against Iraq, as presented by the Cuban government at the United Nations. $10.95. Also available in Spanish.

Art and Revolution

Writings on Literature, Politics, and Culture

LEON TROTSKY

One of the outstanding revolutionary leaders of the 20th century discusses questions of literature, art, and culture in a period of capitalist decline and working-class struggle. In these writings, Trotsky examines the place and aesthetic autonomy of art and artistic expression in the struggle for a new, socialist society. $20.95

The Jewish Question

A Marxist Interpretation

ABRAM LEON

Traces the historical rationalizations of anti-Semitism to the fact that Jews — in the centuries preceding the domination of industrial capitalism — were forced to become a "people-class" of merchants and moneylenders. Leon explains why the propertied rulers incite renewed Jew-hatred today. $17.95

Feminism and the Marxist Movement

MARY-ALICE WATERS

Since the founding of the modern revolutionary workers movement nearly 150 years ago, Marxists have championed the struggle for women's rights and explained the economic roots in class society of women's oppression. $3.50